P9-DEF-083

Before *and After* CHRISTMAS

Activities and Ideas for Advent and Epiphany

By Debbie Trafton O'Neal
Illustrated by David LaRochelle

AUGSBURG • MINNEAPOLIS

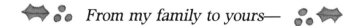 *From my family to yours—*

*May your Advent be filled with anticipation,
May your Christmas be filled with joy,
And may the light of Epiphany bless your family
throughout the year.*

BEFORE AND AFTER CHRISTMAS
Ideas and Activities for Advent and Epiphany

Scripture quotations unless otherwise noted are from the Holy Bible: New International Version. Copyright © 1978 New York International Bible Society. Used by permission of Zondervan Bible Publishers.

Library of Congress Cataloging-in-Publication Data

O'Neal, Debbie Trafton
    Before and after Christmas : ideas and activities for Advent and Epiphany / by Debbie Trafton O'Neal ; illustrated by David LaRochelle.
      p.   cm.
    ISBN 0-8066-2534-1 (alk. paper)
    1. Advent. 2. Christmas. 3. Epiphany season. 4. Family—Religious life. 5. Christmas education—Home training.
6. Christian life—Lutheran authors.   I. Title.
BV40.O57   1991
249—dc20   91-9988
                                  CIP

Manufactured in the U.S.A.   AF 9-2534

95   94   6   7   8   9   10

HOW TO USE THIS BOOK

Advent, the four weeks before Christmas, is a rich season often swallowed up by the world's commercialism. In the same way, the season of Christmas, the twelve days from Christmas Day to Epiphany on January 6, is also lost as people return to "business as usual."

Many of the people I know and have met through my Advent workshops have echoed my thoughts—there must be alternatives to the hectic pace of this time of year. If you have thought the same thing, this book is for you. Through family activities, family time, and family fun, this book gives direction to help us focus more on the true meaning of the days before and after Christmas.

When we take time to prepare, reflect, and renew ourselves during Advent, we eagerly await the birth of Jesus, God's greatest gift to us. These four weeks help us truly celebrate the gift of God's Son on Christmas Day and the days following.

Although this book is intended primarily for families, anyone will benefit from using it, especially those who work with children. It contains information about the history and traditions of the seasons of Advent, Christmas, and Epiphany, as well as symbols and their meanings, the stories of the seasons, and activities for each day up to Epiphany.

Read through the entire book, then decide how you will use it. For instance, if you have small children you may want to extend activities to more than one day. Or you may want to switch activities from one day to another, depending on the amount of time you will have and the type of activity. Don't feel you have to do everything! There are enough ideas here to keep a family busy for several Christmas seasons.

As you plan, keep in mind these things:
- Choose a regular time and place to meet together each day.
- Involve your children in the planning and preparation for each day's activity.
- Read through all directions carefully before you begin. Supplies needed are listed at the beginning of each activity. Most supplies are readily available and you may already have them on hand.
- Take turns reading each day's Bible passage, then spend time reflecting on the text and discussing it together as a family. Even young children will benefit from hearing the Bible reading and talking about it, and a moment of family prayer that relates to the passage and to your own family concerns for the day will be meaningful to all.

3

ADVENT

History and traditions

The word *advent* means "coming." As Christians we know and celebrate this season of the church year as a time to prepare, reflect, and acknowledge our gift of salvation through God's Son, Jesus. In addition, during the Advent season Christians anticipate the promised second coming of Christ.

The season of Advent has evolved throughout history to the four weeks that we know today. Before the Christian church began, Jewish customs placed the new year in the spring. During the first years of the Christian church, those who followed Jesus' teachings continued this tradition. Observances and traditions changed gradually throughout the years, and the celebration of Christ's birth was eventually tied to a midwinter celebration and the beginning of the new year. By the 4th or 5th century, Christmas was established as a religious festival that signified the church year had begun.

In the year A.D. 529, Emperor Justinian declared December 25 a civic holiday as well as a religious holiday. Then in A.D. 567, the Council of Tours established the period of Advent as a time of fasting before Christmas Day. Those who wished to join the Christian church were urged to fast for that period, preparing themselves mentally and physically.

Today the season of Advent is observed for four weeks, although when it was first established, the season was anywhere from three to seven weeks long. Some people think of the four Sundays during Advent as corresponding to the four ways Jesus comes to us: "in the flesh" (at his birth); "in the mind" (when we acknowledge Jesus as our Savior); "in death" (through Jesus' death, we receive eternal life); and "in majesty" (Jesus' coming at the end of time).

Others reflect on Jesus' birth and on his second coming, on John the Baptist who prepared the way for Christ, and on Mary, Jesus' mother and God's obedient servant.

Advent is still observed as the beginning of the church year. The dates change from year to year, the first Sunday in Advent falling on the Sunday nearest November 30. Depending on which day Christmas Eve falls, the season can last from 23 to 28 days.

The use of color has always played a significant part in the observation of church seasons. White was the color used for the entire church year until the 12th century when other colors have been recorded as being used. Purple was originally used for both the season of Advent and the season of Lent, but more recently the color blue has become the symbolic color for Advent. Blue represents "hope" and the joyful anticipation we have as we wait to celebrate Christ's birth on Christmas Day.

Counting the days

Counting the days and weeks is one way to build anticipation for Christmas Day, the celebration of Christ's birth. There are many ways to do this, perhaps the most well known being an Advent calendar or an Advent wreath. You can purchase or make your own Advent calendar, and several Advent wreath suggestions are included here for your family to make and use. (The history and significance of the Advent wreath is found on page 7.) Choose one of the following ideas to use in counting down the days to Christmas.

Evergreen wreaths

A preformed ring, grapevine, or straw wreath can be used as the base for your Advent wreath. Wrap colorful ribbons or cording around the base, then space four candles evenly around the ring. Arrange evergreens on the wreath, covering the base. You may want to add a fifth candle in the center or even in the base itself, to light on Christmas Day and throughout the twelve days of Christmas to Epiphany.

The evergreen branches suggested for use with Advent wreaths are symbolic of the eternal life we have as Christians. For safety's sake, you may want to use silk or plastic evergreen branches with your Advent wreath. If you choose to use real branches, make sure they have been treated with fire-retardant. Your local fire station should be able to tell you how to best do this. Also, never leave candles burning unattended.

Individual wreaths

Individual Advent wreaths can be made by drilling small candle holes in a log round approximately 5″ to 6″ in diameter and about 2″ thick, or into a small Styrofoam round. Insert the candles, putting a small amount of clay in the hole if the candle seems loose, then let each person decorate the wreath with decorations of their own choosing, such as small pinecones, ribbons, bells, or other symbols of the season.

Add-a-hand wreath

Cut the center from a paper plate for the wreath base, perhaps making a wreath for each family member. Each day, as someone does a kind or loving deed for another person, have them trace their handprint onto a piece of green construction paper and glue it to the paper plate. By adding one handprint each day, the wreath should be full by Christmas, becoming a visual reminder of sharing God's love with others during the Advent season.

Yule log

Use a clean log that is approximately 5″ to 7″ in diameter and about 20″ long. Flatten one side of the log so it will not roll. Drill four or five holes about 5″ apart along the top of the log, then insert candles. Evergreens, ribbons, and other decorations can be added if you wish.

Some families who use a Yule log like to save the log from year to year, letting the candle wax drippings accumulate. Other families feel that burning their yule log in a fireplace on Christmas Day is another symbolic way to represent the light Jesus brought into the world.

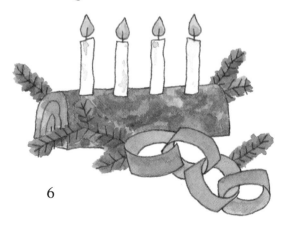

Paper chains

Making paper chains from strips of construction paper is another common way to keep track of the days until Christmas Day. Try this story variation that will also help everyone in the family remember the story of Jesus' birth.

Cut 2″ wide strips of blue paper, one for each day, for the chain. (Blue, the color of Advent, represents "hope.") Write a simple version of the Christmas story, making sure that you have one sentence for each day of Advent. Then print one sentence on each chain link. Staple or tape the chain links together, and hang the chain in a prominent place. Each day during Advent, remove one link, repeating the sentence from that day and the days before. Even small children will be able to tell the Christmas story almost word for word when you reach the last link.

Day 1

"In the beginning was the Word, and the Word was with God, and the Word was God. He was with God in the beginning. Through him all things were made; without him nothing was made that has been made. In him was life, and that life was the light of men. The light shines in the darkness, but the darkness has not understood it."   John 1:1-5

History of the Advent wreath

It is thought that the first Advent wreath originated in Germany or France within the traditions of the Lutheran church. Today the Advent wreath or its variations can be found in many cultures and ethnic communities because of the symbolic way it represents the weeks before Christmas.

The original wreath was most likely a circle of wire, with the circle representing the unending love of God. The evergreens used with the wreath represent the hope of eternal life that all of God's people share. The four candles used in the wreath represent not only the four weeks until Christmas Day, but also the thousands of years people waited for the Messiah to come. As each week's candle was lit, it represented the people's joy and anticipation of the light that came into the world at Jesus' birth.

Although there is no official tradition surrounding the lighting of the Advent wreath candles, different explanations have evolved through time. The most common themes center on the birth and second coming of Christ with the lighting of the first and second candle, then on John the Baptist who prepared the way for Jesus, with the lighting of the third candle, and on Mary, Jesus' mother and God's obedient servant, with the lighting of the last candle. When a fifth candle is added, it represents the true Light come into the world, and is often a much larger candle that will continue to be burned after Christmas Day and into Epiphany.

Other familiar themes include: the first candle as the promise candle or the prophecy candle; the second candle as the Bethlehem candle or the candle of light; the third candle as the candle of love or the shepherd's candle; and the fourth candle as the candle of hope or the angel's candle. Any of these themes may be used with the lighting of the Advent candles, and some people like to change the themes from year to year.

Advent banner

Supplies: (per banner) One 9" x 12" piece of white felt; scraps of blue, purple, pink, and yellow felt; one small piece of Velcro for each flame (4 per banner); 12" long dowel; ribbon or yarn; craft glue or hot glue gun

This banner is a safe way to let young children "light" the candles as they keep track of the weeks until Christmas.

Use scissors to trim one 9" end of the white felt, either with scallops or with a sawtooth edge. Fold the opposite end of the felt piece down 1" to make a casing, then sew or glue the casing seam, making sure to leave enough room for the dowel to fit through. Cut four "candles" from the felt scraps, using either blue or purple for three of the candles and making one candle pink. The candles should be about 4"-5" long and 1½" wide. Cut four flame shapes from the yellow felt. (If you wish, cut holly or evergreen shapes from green felt and add to the base of the candles as well.) Center and glue the candles on the banner, using the pink candle as the third candle. Glue one part of the Velcro fastener to the back of each flame, then the other part of the fastener to the banner above the candle.

Day 2

"Show me your ways, O Lord, teach me your paths." *Psalm 25:4*

Family traditions

With the busy lives that most of us lead today, it is hard, if not almost impossible, to consistently spend time together as a family. Establishing regular family routines, such as sharing at least one meal together a day or having a time for family devotions, can form an important base for positive family relationships and give opportunity to teach children God's truth. Forming traditions that center around special seasons such as Christmas can become one of those memorable bonds that keeps a family close throughout the years. This Advent, consider establishing some family traditions that are meaningful to you.

Our family started a new tradition one year when we cut our own Christmas tree. Near the top of the tree, we found an abandoned bird's nest, which we left in place that year as part of our tree's decorations. When we took our tree down, we carefully wrapped the nest and put it away for the years and Christmas trees to come.

Some traditions in families have been passed down through the generations. Others are planned because of certain circumstances. Keep your eyes and your hearts open for the wonder of those traditions your family may discover this year and in each year to come!

A book of family traditions

Supplies: A notebook.

Create a unique family Advent book to hold special holiday plans and memories from year to year. Include a calendar of events, Christmas card lists, gift ideas, and holiday entertaining menus and recipes in your notebook. Update your book yearly, adding pictures and noting new traditions that your family enjoys.

☆ ADVENT COUNTDOWN! ☆

SUN	MON	TUE	WED	THUR	FRI	SAT
NOV 29	30 PICK UP BOY SCOUT WREATHS	DEC 1 DELIVER WREATHS	2	3	4 ✳ ICE SKATING WITH MORGAN	5 TAKE GRANDMA SHOPPING
6	7	8 BAKE COOKIES!	9	10 MAIL CHRISTMAS CARDS	11	12 1:00 CHRISTMAS PAGEANT REHEARSAL
13 VISIT UNCLE VERTIS	14 DINNER AT THE SUNDELL'S	15	16	17 MARTHA'S CONCERT	18 CAROLING WITH YOUTH GROUP	19 1:00 CHRISTMAS PAGEANT REHEARSAL
20 8:00 CHRISTMAS PAGEANT	21	22	23 😊 6:00 – 9:00 VOLUNTEER AT FOOD SHELF	24 7:00 CANDLELIGHT SERVICE	25 CHRISTMAS!	26

A family calendar

Supplies: A large sheet of paper or poster board; felt-tip pens; stickers.

Make a planning calendar as shown, being sure to leave space to write in the activities for each day. Plan your family calendar for the entire Advent season, printing the dates for special events and get-togethers, family outings, and "things to do" in the calendar spaces. If you like, draw small pictures in some of the spaces to represent the activity. Music notes, for example, could signify a Christmas concert you will be attending. Hang the completed calendar on the refrigerator or some other prominent place in your home so everyone can keep track of the days and their events. Be sure to add events and appointments to the calendar as you become aware of them.

Day 3

"At that time Mary got ready and hurried to a town in the hill country of Judah, where she entered Zechariah's home and greeted Elizabeth. When Elizabeth heard Mary's greeting, the baby leaped in her womb, and Elizabeth was filled with the Holy Spirit."   *Luke 1:39-41*

A special guest

Elizabeth had a special guest come to her home. Mary had important news to share with Elizabeth. Both women were happy to see one another and greeted each other warmly.

During the time around Christmas, we often have guests in our homes. Like Elizabeth, we make them welcome and gladly entertain them. Even children can be part of our hospitality, by greeting visitors at the door, helping serve any refreshments, and taking part in conversations when appropriate. More importantly, we all can share in the good news that Mary brought to Elizabeth—Jesus is coming!

Guest handprint chain

Supplies: Construction paper in assorted colors; scissors; stapler; felt-tip pens.

Give your children a job to do when you have guests coming over during the holiday season. Whenever visitors arrive, have your children help the guests trace their handprints onto a sheet of construction paper and write their names inside the hands. (Some people may even become creative with their handprints, by adding rings or other details.) Then cut out the handprints.

Attach the handprints together with a stapler, adding more handprints each time you have company. Drape the handprint chain in a stair-well, over a railing, or in any entry-way, so that everyone who comes through the door will see it.

Not only will your children be involved with meeting and greeting your guests throughout the holidays, your family will have a visual record of all of the people who came to your home.

Day 4

"A shoot will come up from the stump of Jesse; from his roots a Branch will bear fruit."
Isaiah 11:1

The Jesse tree

The name "Jesse" in Jesse tree refers to King David's father. The text in Isaiah 11:1 tells us that from his stump the Messiah comes. The Jesse tree tradition remembers all those people who went before Jesus and helped to prepare the way.

Although the historical tradition for Christians is to trim a tree on Christmas Eve, it is becoming exceedingly harder and harder to follow this practice in today's world. Some families have adapted the idea of the Jesse tree into their family celebration by putting up their Christmas tree about the middle of Advent, but decorating it with only symbols that represent people from Old Testament stories. The people in these stories are the ones who longed for Christ, the Messiah, to come.

If you and your family decide to try this with your tree this year, you might want to put the Chi Rho, a symbol that represents Christ, on top of the tree. Other symbols that call to mind Jesus, such as the cross or the lamb, could also be added to the tree on Christmas Day or on the 12 days following.

Make your own Jesse tree

Supplies: Small evergreen or other living tree, or a tree branch in a container weighted with sand; blue poster board; construction paper; blue yarn; paper hole punch

Secure the tree or tree branch so that it will not tip over. Read again the explanation of a Jesse tree, then decide what symbols you will use to represent the Old Testament people. Some examples might be: stone tablets for Moses, a ladder and stars for Jacob, a boat for Noah, a big fish for Jonah, or a sheaf of wheat for Ruth. Draw and cut these symbols from construction paper, then mount them on pieces of blue poster board. Punch a hole in the top of each piece and string a length of yarn through the hole to hang it on the tree.

You may want to make this project last for a week or more, taking the time to read or tell the Old Testament stories aloud with your family before you create the Jesse tree ornaments.

Day 5

"Therefore, as God's chosen people, holy and dearly loved, clothe yourselves with compassion, kindness, humility, gentleness and patience. . . . And whatever you do, whether in word or deed, do it all in the name of the Lord Jesus, giving thanks to God the Father through him." Colossians 3:12,17

Saint Nicholas Eve, December 5

Saint Nicholas has been known and loved for centuries. He was born in Asia Minor (now Turkey) in the fourth century A.D., and it is believed he became a bishop in the church at a very young age. Throughout his life, Saint Nicholas was known for his compassion, kindness, and generosity. Many stories of his good works circulated throughout the towns and villages in the area in which he lived. Some of them have been passed down through the ages.

The most familiar story of Saint Nicholas involves a family with three daughters. The family was so poor that the eldest daughter was going to be sold into slavery. Nicholas, unseen, dropped a bag of gold one night through an open window, thus providing a marriage dowry for the daughter. In time, he dropped another bag of gold through an open window for the second daughter's marriage dowry. Again, no one saw Nicholas. But when he tried to secretly leave a bag of gold for the third daughter, someone saw him. Nicholas begged the person not to tell what he had seen, but the story of his generosity spread. Ever since that time, children have eagerly waited for gifts from Saint Nicholas.

On the evening of December 5, many children in European countries wait for a visit from Saint Nicholas. Sometimes he visits the children's homes while they are still awake, finding out if they have been good and leaving them special treats. Other times, Saint Nicholas visits the children's homes when they are fast asleep, and in the morning the children wake to find the presents he has left for them.

Saint Nicholas is the real person around whom our tradition of Santa Claus has evolved. The debate between the emphasis on Santa Claus at Christmas and the emphasis on the birth of Jesus is one that families need to settle on their own. Surely as Christians we know the true meaning of Christmas is the birth of God's Son, Jesus. By focusing on the real Saint Nicholas and stressing that he acted out of Christian love, we can shift the emphasis away from Santa Claus and commercialism. Better yet, we can help our children to know and understand that we value God's gift of Jesus over the gifts of any other.

Saint Nicholas mobile

Supplies: Red, white, and black construction paper or poster board; thread; hole punch; scissors; glue.

This mobile can be used as a tree ornament, package decoration, or you may just hang it from the ceiling. Cut the mobile shapes from construction paper or poster board, enlarging the pieces to any size you wish. Cut *two* of each shape so that a length of thread can be inserted between the shapes when they are glued together.

Once you have cut out the pieces, glue one white circle and one white rectangle to each of the red triangles to make two hat pieces. Then glue black circles (eyes) to the white face rectangles. Punch out two red circles with your hole punch. Glue them to the face pieces where the nose should be.

When the glue is dry, assemble the mobile by arranging one beard, face, and hat piece wrong side up as shown, leaving about ¼" space between the pieces. Glue a 14" length of thread along the center of the pieces, making a loop at the top and gluing it inside

the hat for a hanger. Glue the remaining pieces over the top of the thread, matching each piece carefully, and making sure to keep the thread loop on the outside when you glue the hat pieces together.

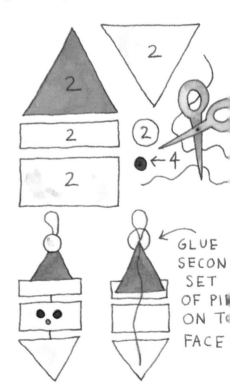

14

Day 6 ✗ ✗ ✗ ✗ ✗ ✗ ✗ ✗ ✗

"This will be a sign to you: You will find a baby wrapped in cloths and lying in a manger."
Luke 2:12

Signs of Christmas

The season of Advent is full of signs, all pointing to the baby the shepherds found lying in a manger. Take time today to note the signs around your home that point to the baby Jesus. Have you made an Advent wreath? Do you add an ornament to your Jesse tree each day? What other seasonal items decorate your home and remind you of the baby Jesus?

Also take time to think of the signs in your life that point to the manger. Are you preparing your heart for the coming of the Savior, or have the pressures of the season pushed Jesus aside? A good way to focus again on the manger is by creating a visual reminder of it—you can make your own family's manger scene.

A wood block nativity

Supplies: Wood blocks (made from two-by-fours) ranging in size from 5″ to 10″; felt pieces in assorted colors; assorted beads; glitter or jewelry findings; white craft glue.

This set of wood and felt nativity blocks is especially appropriate for families with young children. Decide which figures you want to have in your nativity scene and cut one block for each figure. Sand the wood blocks

well to eliminate slivers, and round the corners slightly for safety.

In addition to Mary, Joseph, and the baby Jesus, you might want to add the wise men, one or more shepherds, an angel, and some sheep and other animals that may have been in the stable. Adapt the simple drawings here for your figures. Cut the body shapes from felt and glue onto the appropriate wood block. Then layer different garments, hair or beads, faces, and other features onto the basic body shape. Add sequins and other decorations to the figures as you wish.

Day 7

"The people walking in darkness have seen a great light; on those living in the land of the shadow of death, a light has dawned."   Isaiah 9:2

The legend of the lightning bug

Long ago, there was a small bug who lived in the town of Bethlehem. One night, the bug flew into a warm stable because he was cold. He settled down to sleep in a dark corner, and the rustling of the hay and the quiet chewing of the cows lulled the bug to sleep.

But then the small bug heard voices in the stable. "What's this? Who is talking?" thought the bug. "This is a cattle barn!"

The voices the little bug heard were the voices of Mary and Joseph, who had come to Bethlehem to pay their taxes. The town of Bethlehem was so crowded with other people who had come to pay their taxes that this was the only place left for anyone to sleep.

The small bug decided he didn't mind if Mary and Joseph shared the stable with the cows and him, and he quickly went back to sleep. Then, once again, the little bug was awakened.

This time, a soft golden light filled the stable, and he could see Mary holding a little baby in her arms. Then the voices of angels began singing with joy, "Glory to God in the highest!"

While the little bug watched from his corner, one of the angel's crowns slipped. The angel took off the crown and when she did, a sparkling emerald dropped out and fell on the small bug.

"Ouch!" the bug said to himself. "That hurts!"

But the angel never noticed the small bug. She picked up the emerald and put it back into the crown with the others.

After the angels finished singing, they left the stable. While Mary, Joseph, and the baby rested, the little bug thought about everything he had just seen and heard. When he finally settled down again to go back to sleep, the bug noticed a soft green light shining from the place on his body where the emerald had dropped. Now the bug had his very own light!

Ever since that time, the little bug and all other bugs like him have had their very own lights to shine in the dark night sky. We call these bugs "lightning bugs" or "fireflies" and they remind us of the night Jesus was born in a dark stable.

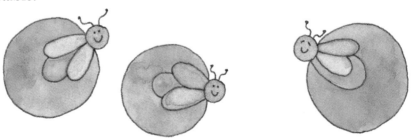

Luminaries

Supplies: Lunch-size paper bags; scissors or a paper hole punch; votive candles and candle holders; sand.

Cut or punch designs in the paper bags as shown. Set the candle holder and candles in the bags and anchor the bags with a handful of sand. Place the luminaries along a sidewalk or pathway leading to your front door when you are expecting guests or on Christmas Eve.

"Here's Baby Jesus" fingerplay

Here's baby Jesus. (*Hold up one index finger.*)
I'll put him to bed (*Lay index finger in other hand.*)
And cover him up, (*Fold fingers over index finger.*)
All but his head. (*Leave tip of index finger out.*)
And if he should wake, I'll put him right here (*Put index finger to shoulder as if comforting a baby.*)
And pretend that I'm Mary, who loved him so dear. (*Rock an imaginary baby in your arms.*)

Day 8

"In those days Caesar Augustus issued a decree that a census should be taken of the entire Roman world. (This was the first census that took place while Quirinius was governor of Syria.) And everyone went to his own town to register. So Joseph also went up from the town of Nazareth in Galilee to Judea, to Bethlehem the town of David."   Luke 2:1-4

Across the Miles

Joseph and Mary had to make a trip to Joseph's hometown. Though it was not far in today's terms, it was a difficult journey for them, especially for Mary who was about to give birth to Jesus.

At Christmastime, many of us also travel back to our hometowns to be with those we love. Sometimes, it is not possible to gather physically with our extended families, but we can still remain close across the miles with a few thoughtful gestures and with loving thoughts. Here are some ideas to stay in touch with relatives during the holiday season and throughout the year.

Personal postcards

Buy pre-stamped postcards at the post office, then glue a standard print of a favorite family snapshot on the front. Send your Christmas message now, and a monthly message during the rest of the year, using a new picture each time.

Sharing art

Rather than discarding your children's artwork for which you no longer have refrigerator space, write letters on the backs of it to send to friends, grandparents, and other relatives. Let the children write messages of their own on the backs as well.

Taped messages

Record a dinner conversation or some of the songs or poems your child has been learning and send it to a relative who lives far away. If one of your children has just begun learning to read, send a tape of him or her reading too.

Day 9

"For to us a child is born, to us a son is given, and the government will be on his shoulders. And he will be called Wonderful Counselor, Mighty God, Everlasting Father, Prince of Peace."
Isaiah 9:6

A king born in a stable

To us a child was born, in a stable, with animals, and ordinary shepherds as his first visitors. It is hard for us to imagine such a humble beginning for so great a King. But it was the setting God chose for the birth of the Son.

The manger scene has become a treasured symbol of Christmas. Nearly every home has one. It is believed that the first manger scene was set up in Italy by Francis of Assisi, and it contained real animals and life-sized figures. The practice of real-life nativity scenes spread throughout southern Europe. Later, people began to make miniature manger scenes that could be set up in their homes.

Many communities around the world continue to set up living nativity scenes at Christmas. Check to see if some church in your community does that. If none does, perhaps you could start the tradition.

A living nativity scene

You will need: A stable, shed, or frame to use for the background; a bright light for the star; fencing of some sort; straw or hay; live animals such as cows, sheep, and chickens; willing people; costumes as desired.

Set up the stable scene in an enclosed or temporarily fenced area. Let the animals become accustomed to the surroundings before the nights when you all take part. Decide on which nights you will offer the living nativity scene, and advertise the times on local radio and in your community newspaper. It is a good idea to have shifts of one hour each for the participants, especially if you live in a place where the weather may not cooperate, or where it is very cold.

Provide refreshments for the people who are playing the parts and be sure to take pictures!

Day 10

"When they had seen him, they spread the word concerning what had been told them about this child, and all who heard it were amazed at what the shepherds said to them." Luke 2:17-18

Spread the news

The shepherds gladly spread the news of Jesus' birth throughout the countryside, telling everyone they met about the angels' message and the baby in the manger. Like the shepherds, we too are messengers at Christmas, spreading the news to people far and near, that Jesus is born.

This year, as you send off your holiday greetings, share the word of joy that comes with the birth of the Savior. Spread the news!

Use the following suggestion to create special greeting cards to send to friends and relatives.

Pop-up cards

Supplies: Construction paper or poster board; scissors; glue.

To make the bell card as shown here, first cut a piece of construction paper or poster board to 5½" high x 7¼" wide. Fold in half for the card. Fold in half a 3½" x 4" piece of contrasting paper for the bells. Transfer the bell designs as shown and cut out. Fold the hinges as indicated.

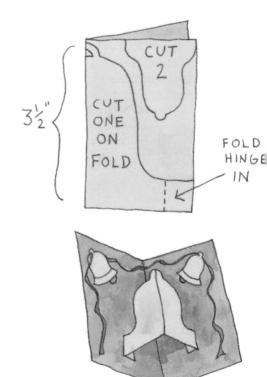

Finish by unfolding the card and large bell and gluing only the hinges of the bell to the inside of the card. The bell should lie flat when the card is fully opened. Glue the two smaller bells inside the card. Draw additional decorations as desired. Make sure the glue is dry before closing the card.

Make other cards using any of the symbols on pages 30-31. Simply add hinges, fold, and score the shapes as described above.

Day 11 ſ ſ ſ ſ ſ ſ ſ ſ ſ ſ

"And there were shepherds living out in the fields nearby, keeping watch over their flocks at night."   *Luke 2:8*

The legend of the Glastonbury thorn

There is an old legend that tells us the story of a thorn tree that grows in Glastonbury, England. In the first years of the Christian church, Joseph of Arimathea traveled from his home in Jerusalem to Glastonbury. Joseph was the man who had taken the body of Jesus down from the cross and laid it to rest in the tomb.

As the legend goes, when Joseph of Arimathea arrived in Glastonbury just before Christmas, he planted in the ground the hawthorn walking staff that he had brought with him from Jerusalem, claiming the area as holy ground for the Lord. By Christmas Eve, the walking staff had taken root and burst into bloom. Each year that followed, the staff continued to bloom on Christmas Eve, and people for centuries have traveled to see it.

During Puritan times, the original hawthorn staff was cut down, but grafts and cuttings had fortunately taken root in nearby ground. Even today a thorn tree that came from a shoot of Joseph's staff can be found blooming on Christmas Eve in the abbey grounds at Glastonbury.

Shepherd's staff cookies

Ingredients:
½ cup margarine, softened
½ cup shortening
1 cup confectioner's sugar
1 egg
1½ teaspoons almond extract
1 teaspoon vanilla
2½ cups flour
1 teaspoon salt
½ teaspoon red food coloring
½ cup crushed peppermint candy
½ cup granulated sugar

Heat oven to 375°. Mix together margarine, shortening, confectioner's sugar, egg, vanilla, and almond extract. Blend in flour and salt, then divide the dough in half. Blend red food coloring into one half and set the other aside.

Roll 1 teaspoon of dough from each half into a 4″ rope. Place the two different colored ropes side by side, press together lightly, and twist. Place on an ungreased baking sheet. Curve the top down to form the crook.

Bake for 9 minutes or until set and a very light brown. Mix the peppermint candy and granulated sugar and immediately sprinkle the cookies with it. Remove from baking sheet and let cool. Makes 4 dozen.

Day 12

"After they had heard the king, they went on their way, and the star they had seen in the east went ahead of them until it stopped over the place where the child was." *Matthew 2:9*

The legend of the candles on the Christmas tree

The legend of the candles on the Christmas tree comes from the country of Germany and is told about Martin Luther, the leader of the Reformation over 500 years ago.

One cold, clear December night, Martin Luther was returning to his home. Part of his path took him through the woods, where he could see the stars twinkling and shining in the night sky. As he walked along, Martin Luther noticed how brightly the stars shone through the snow-covered branches of the fir trees in the forest. The stars twinkled and shone so brightly they were like diamonds in the night! Martin Luther wished he could share his joy and wonder at this beautiful sight with the people he loved most—his wife and their children. Then he had an idea.

Martin Luther cut a small evergreen tree and took it home with him. At home, he tied small white candles to the tree's branches and when the candles were lit, he told his family about what he had seen in the woods. Martin Luther shared his view of God's creation and the great gift of God's Son who brought light into the world for all to see. We continue the tradition today by bringing evergreen trees into our homes and stringing lights through the branches.

Symbol tree skirt

Supplies: 1¾ yards of 60″ wide green felt; assorted colors of felt for symbol shapes; craft glue; rick-rack or pompom fringe (optional); scissors; tracing paper; pencil.

Cut a 60″ diameter circle from the green felt, then fold it into quarters with the edges even. Draw a 1¾″ radius from the center, then cut all the layers along the pencil line to make a round center opening. Cut along one fold only to make the back opening for the tree skirt.

If you plan to put rick-rack or pompom fringe on the tree skirt, stitch it on before you begin adding the symbol shapes.

Trace and cut patterns for Advent and Christmas symbols (see pp. 30-31), enlarging them to whatever size you wish. Cut the symbols from felt, and lay out your design to fit around the tree skirt. Affix the symbols in place with craft glue.

This is a project that you may want to extend for more than one day. You may even continue adding symbols to

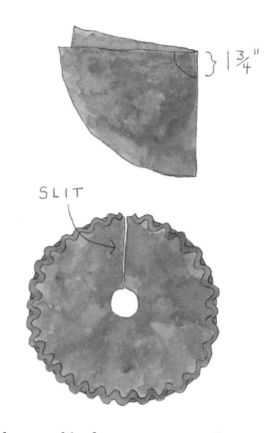

} 1 ¾″

SLIT

the tree skirt from year to year. For example, you might choose one symbol per year and research it before adding it to your tree skirt.

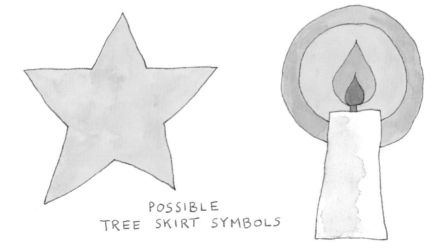

POSSIBLE
TREE SKIRT SYMBOLS

23

Day 13

"Suddenly a great company of the heavenly host appeared with the angel, praising God and saying, 'Glory to God in the highest, and on earth peace to men on whom his favor rests.'"   *Luke 2:13-14*

The legend of Santa Lucia

There is a legend in Sweden about a young saint named Lucia that people still use as the basis for the celebration *Luciadagen* or Santa Lucia Day.

The legend tells us that there was once a time of great hunger in Sweden. During that time, Santa Lucia appeared with food for everyone in the country. When she appeared, her head was surrounded by a great halo of light.

Tradition states that early in the morning on December 13, in homes throughout Sweden, the oldest daughter carries a special breakfast of coffee and sweet bread to her parents' bedroom. Usually she is dressed in a simple white gown tied with a red sash, and she wears a crown of evergreen branches with seven candles in it. Her sisters and brothers follow her, all dressed in white.

In many towns, a young woman is chosen as the Santa Lucia to carry the coffee and sweetbreads to each home. She is followed by carolers carrying candles.

Even if your background is not Swedish, a special breakfast during the season of Advent would be a welcome way to start a new day, and may even become one of your family's favorite traditions!

Scandinavian woven hearts

Supplies: 2 sheets of glossy paper or construction paper (1 each of two different colors—red and white are traditional); scissors; glue

Cut a 7" x 2" strip from each color of paper. Fold the strips in half, then round the ends and cut slits as indicated in diagram 1. Weave the two sections together as indicated in diagram 2, weaving each strip one at a time through and over each other. Make a handle from one of the colors of the heart, gluing it in place on the inside of the basket. Fill the heart with small candies, raisins or nuts and hang it as an ornament on your tree or share it with a neighbor on Santa Lucia Day.

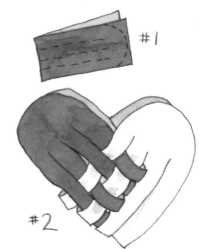

#1

#2

Day 14 JOY • JOY • JOY • JOY • JOY • JOY

"Shout with joy to God, all the earth! Sing to the glory of his name; offer him glory and praise! Say to God, 'How awesome are your deeds! So great is your power that your enemies cringe before you. All the earth bows down to you; they sing praise to you, they sing praise to your name.'" Psalm 66:1-4

"Joy" around the world

The third Sunday in Advent is known as *Gaudete* or "joyful" Sunday. On this Sunday in Advent, people around the world remember with great joy the love that God has for them and they look forward with joyful anticipation to the celebration of Jesus' birth on Christmas Day.

Spreading joy

Here are some different ways to write and say the word *joy* in languages from many countries around the world. How many of them can you learn? Spread some joy by including these words on cards and wrapping paper you create (see p. 41).

Language	Write it	Say it
French	*joie*	zhwah
German	*Freude*	FROY-deh
Spanish	*alegría*	ah-leh-GREE-ah
Italian	*gioia*	DJOH-yah
Norwegian	*glede*	glyeh-deh
Swedish	*fröjd*	frayd
Dutch	*vreujde*	frukh-deh
Greek	*chará*	khah-RAH
Gaelic	*ātas*	OH-hass
Hawaiian	*olioli*	OH-lee-OH-lee
Polish	*radość*	rah-DOHSHT'CH

Day 15

"Thanks be to God for his indescribable gift!" 2 Corinthians 9:15

The legend of the poinsettia

A Mexican Christmas legend tells us a story about the beautiful, red poinsettia, known as the flower of Christmas.

One Christmas Eve long ago, a young girl named Lola was outside the church praying. She was very sad because she did not have any gift to give to the baby Jesus in the manger. As Lola watched all the other people from the village carry flowers into the church, tears began to fall from her eyes.

"Please, Lord," Lola prayed, "help me! I don't have any gift for the baby Jesus, not even a flower to show how much I love him."

Suddenly a bright light surrounded Lola, and she covered her eyes in fear. But she peeked between her fingers when she heard a kind voice say, "Don't cry, Lola! The Holy Child Jesus knows that you love him. He sees all the kind and loving things you do for others. Go and gather those plants growing near the road and take them to the manger."

Lola knew the voice was the voice of her guardian angel. But even so, she wasn't sure about the plants the angel was talking about.

"Those plants are only weeds," she said.

"Ah," said the angel with a smile, "that's what people think! But weeds are only plants for which people have not yet discovered God's purpose."

Lola dried her tears and bent eagerly to pick the plants as the angel had instructed. Then she carried the plants into the church and laid them proudly with all of the beautiful flowers the other villagers had left by the manger.

Suddenly, everyone in the church gasped in surprise. Lola's weeds had turned a crimson shade of red! Ever since the day Lola brought her gift to the manger, these weeds have been known in Mexico as *flores de la Noche Buena*—the Christmas flowers.

Window paintings

Supplies: Felt-tip pens; large pieces of paper such as shelf paper or brown paper bags; paintbrushes; dry tempera paint; bowls or other containers to mix paints in; masking tape; newspaper.

Cut sheets of paper slightly smaller than your window panes. (You may have to tape several pieces of paper together first.) Work together to draw window-size holiday art such as the beautiful poinsettia, or scenes from the first Christmas or from your own holiday activities. You need only draw the outlines; you will fill in the color later when painting.

Once you are pleased with your designs, tape the paper, with the drawing facing in, to the outside of the window. Lay newspaper on the floor inside and add extra tape to the window frame for protection.

Mix your paints fairly thick to prevent dripping and begin painting on the inside of the window, using the drawings as patterns to fill in. Begin with the lightest colors and smaller detailed areas, then fill in the larger and darker areas and background. Allow the paint to dry before adding different colors, to avoid running the colors together.

In the daylight, the painted windows will glow like stained glass, and at night the colors will appear jewel-like against the dark sky.

Day 16

"Praise the Lord, O my soul; all my inmost being, praise his holy name. Praise the Lord, O my soul, and forget not all his benefits. He forgives all my sins and heals my diseases; he redeems my life from the pit and crowns me with love and compassion."   Psalm 103:1-3

The legend of the holly

According to one legend, the crown of thorns that Jesus wore at his crucifixion was made from holly branches and leaves twined together in a circle. The legend says that as soldiers pressed the crown into Jesus' brow, the white berries on the holly turned a brilliant red. To this day, the holly's berries are bright red, reminding us of the blood Jesus shed for us.

The use of holly in wreaths and other decorations at Christmas, the day of Jesus' birth, foreshadows his suffering and death. We are reminded that the baby born in Bethlehem grew to be the man who was crucified for our sake. Because of Jesus' death and resurrection, we have been redeemed, and crowned with his love and compassion. When we hang wreaths in our homes at Christmas, we can give thanks for Jesus' never-ending love for us.

Mini-wreath cookies

These colorful cookies resemble miniature holly wreaths when done.

Ingredients:
30 regular-size marshmallows
½ cup margarine
1 teaspoon vanilla
1 teaspoon green food coloring
3½ cups cereal flakes

small red cinnamon candies
red licorice whips or tube of ready-made red frosting (for ribbon)
several round plastic lids (like those on margarine containers)

Mix the marshmallows, vanilla, food coloring, and margarine in a double boiler or microwave oven, stirring until just melted. Gradually stir in cereal flakes, making sure all flakes are covered with marshmallow mixture. Form cereal mixture into a wreath shape on the plastic lid. Add red candy berries, and form a piece of red licorice whip into a bow, or pipe one on with red frosting. Let cookie set before removing it from the lid.

Day 17

"Therefore the Lord himself will give you a sign: The virgin will be with child and will give birth to a son, and will call him Immanuel." Isaiah 7:14

Signs and symbols

Signs and symbols are important in our lives. They point the way for us or help explain things. They use few words, if any, to get their point across. In fact, young children can identify symbols for many things long before they are able to read. Signs and symbols can lead us all to a deeper understanding of something.

The Christian faith uses symbols in an integral way—in worship, on banners and jewelry, and in language that helps us better understand God's Word.

The seasons of the church year have many rich images connected to them. The symbols found on pages 30-31 are ones that we often see and use during the seasons of Advent, Christmas, and Epiphany.

Symbol place mats

Make a set of festive place mats for your family to use at mealtime. Instructions for making two different kinds are included below.

Supplies: Construction paper in assorted colors; clear adhesive-backed paper or wax paper; scissors; newspaper; iron.

Choose symbols from pages 30-31 to cut from different colors of construction paper. Include a variety of different symbols in different colors for each place mat.

If you are using clear adhesive-backed paper for your place mats, lay the completed symbols on a contrasting color of construction paper, then cover the entire sheet of paper with the clear adhesive paper.

If you are using wax paper, sandwich the paper symbols between two sheets of wax paper, then the wax paper between several thicknesses of newspaper. Iron over the entire surface with an iron set on medium, fusing the wax paper together around the symbols. After the paper cools, you can trim the place mat edges in a scallop or zig-zag design if you wish.

The open Bible represents the Good News.

The crown reminds us of Jesus, our king.

Jesus was born in a manger.

The key represents Jesus as the key to eternal life.

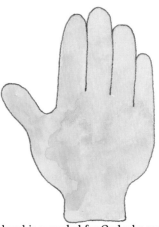

A hand is a symbol for God who reaches out to us in love. It also represents God the creator.

Jesus is the lamb of God, who takes away our sins.

People hand-in-hand symbolize our need to work together, love one another, and be a part of God's family.

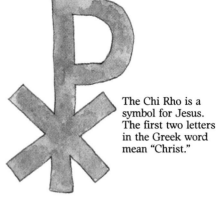

The fish was the symbol used by early Christians to help identify who Jesus' followers were.

The Chi Rho is a symbol for Jesus. The first two letters in the Greek word mean "Christ."

A dove represents peace. Jesus came to bring peace to the world.

The globe reminds us that God's love reaches out to all people and reminds us of our call to also reach out to others.

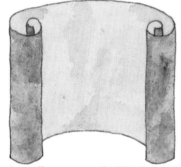

A scroll represents the Word of God.

The star represents the prophecy that was fulfilled in Jesus. A large star surrounded by a cluster of many smaller stars reminds us of the promise that Abraham would have many descendants.

The angel reminds us of the great joy Christmas brings to us.

31

Day 18

"An angel of the Lord appeared to them, and the glory of the Lord shone around them, and they were terrified." — Luke 2:9

The legend of the Christmas angel

Many people place an angel at the top of their Christmas tree to remind them of the special part the angels played the night Jesus was born.

Legend tells us that each year the angels weave new cloth for the garments that the Christ child will wear when he brings his gifts from heaven to all the people on earth. The threads of the garments that the angels weave are said to be the prayers of the children who love Jesus and his heavenly Father. Remember the story of the angels and the cloth woven of children's prayers when you say your prayers tonight.

Three-dimensional angel

Supplies: Construction paper or decorative paper (wallpaper or heavy giftwrap); scissors; pencil; stapler; hole punch; yarn or ribbon.

Enlarge the angel pattern on page 31 to whatever size you wish, then cut two pieces from heavy paper. Fold each piece in half lengthwise, then open up flat. Place one piece on top of the other, and staple along the center fold line. Open the angel so it will stand. If you wish to hang the angel, punch a hole in the top and string a piece of yarn or ribbon through.

Angel in the round

Supplies: White construction paper; scissors; tape; glue; felt-tip pens (optional).

Enlarge the angel pattern shown below. Cut out along the lines, then bend the head gently away from the body. To complete the angel, fold the wings back until they overlap slightly. Glue, tape, or staple them together as shown. You might draw on features before attaching the wings together.

TWO PIECES STAPLED TOGETHER

32

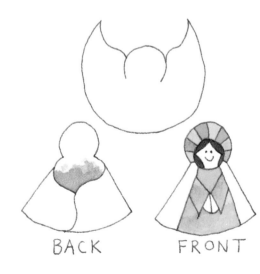

BACK   FRONT

Day 19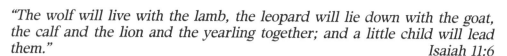

"The wolf will live with the lamb, the leopard will lie down with the goat, the calf and the lion and the yearling together; and a little child will lead them."

Isaiah 11:6

The legend of the animals' Christmas

Many countries have different legends that tell of the animals' part in the first Christmas. Because Jesus was born in a stable, with a manger full of hay for a bed, people around the world remember animals in a special way at Christmas.

One old legend tells us that every Christmas Eve, just as the clock strikes midnight, all the barnyard animals receive the gift of speech so that they can kneel again to tell the story of Jesus' holy birth.

Other stories in folklore tell us that all God's creatures honored the baby Jesus in their own way. Bees hummed their own tunes of praise, while spiders spun fine webs of gossamer on Christmas trees. At the touch of the baby Jesus' hands, the threads of the spider's web turned to silver.

And in every country around the world, the bearers of Christmas gifts have their own animal helpers. Saint Nicholas rides a fine white horse while the Three Kings ride horses or camels. Even Santa Claus with his sleigh has a team of flying reindeer to guide him through the night.

If you have pets or animal visitors, think about the ways that your family can remember them in special ways this Advent season.

PRETZEL FENCE

Gingerbread stable

Supplies: One pint-size milk carton for each stable; masking tape; graham crackers; icing (see recipe below); raisins, nuts and small candies for decorations; animal cookies.

Make a gingerbread stable filled with animal cookies! You can make other gingerbread-style buildings by following the same basic instructions.

Make icing by combining 3 egg whites, 1 teaspoon cream of tartar, and 1 lb. confectioner's (powdered) sugar.

Wash and shake out the empty carton, and tape the top shut. Spread a thin coating of icing over the carton, then press graham crackers onto the icing, completely covering the carton. Fill in any spaces with additional icing. Let the icing dry for at least 1 hour or overnight.

To decorate the stable, spread more icing on the crackers and add raisins, nuts or small candies to make windows and doorways. If you can find star-shaped candy, attach a piece to the top of the roof with icing.

Spread a small amount of icing on the backs of several animal cookies and press them onto the sides of the stable as well.

Day 20

"For God so loved the world that he gave his one and only Son, that whoever believes in him shall not perish but have eternal life."   *John 3:16*

The season of love

A familiar carol proclaims, "Love came down at Christmas." Indeed, Valentine's Day is not the only holiday that centers on love. Love is foremost in our thoughts at Christmas. It is the season of love.

At Christmas we focus on the love we have for family and good friends and especially on the great love God had for us in sending Jesus. We are commanded by Jesus to "Love each other, as I have loved you" (John 15:12). Besides loving our family and friends, we are to reach out in love to our neighbors—people whom we might not even know. God's love was so great that God gave us the Son. We can, with thankful hearts, give of ourselves.

Adopt a family

Not everyone is guaranteed to have a "Merry Christmas." There are many people for whom Christmas is a hardship. They don't have the means to celebrate in the usual fashion. They often must depend on the goodwill of others.

Check with your pastor or a local community agency to see if there is a family you could "adopt" for this holiday season. If possible, try to be matched with a family similar in size and ages to your own. As you shop for your holiday meals, remember this family and buy food for them. You might even want to include the recipes you will be using for them to try. As you shop for gifts for your family, buy two of everything, especially for the children in the family. Receiving the "latest" toy or article of clothing means a lot to children who may not be used to having much.

Whatever you do for another family during this season of the year will make the idea of "giving" a lot more meaningful for you. Isn't this what Christmas is all about?

Christmas mail prayers

Set aside any Christmas cards or greetings that you receive each day, and read them at a mealtime when your entire family will be together. Include the people who have sent greetings to you in your prayers, asking God to bless their holiday season and the coming year.

Day 21

"We must help the weak, remembering the words the Lord Jesus himself said: 'It is more blessed to give than to receive.' "   Acts 20:35

Good King Wenceslas

Most everyone knows the familiar carol "Good King Wenceslas," and how the good king and his page braved the bitter cold of winter to bring food and firewood to a poor peasant. But few may know that this good man really once existed.

Wenceslas was born in 924, the son of King Vratislav of Bohemia. The kingdom was in great unrest, and King Vratislav himself was murdered. The young Wenceslas was to become king, but it was feared that his life was in danger too. To protect him, his grandmother sent him to a monastery in the country. While at the monastery, Wenceslas learned much about the Christian life and grew to be a devout follower of Jesus. Meanwhile, his brother Boleslas tried to take the throne. He was an evil man, and he treated the people of the kingdom cruelly.

When Wenceslas returned to the capital from his time in the monastery, he was distressed to find the poor people being so ill-treated. He strove to bring his people to the Christian faith and for a time there was peaceful rule in the land, and the people prospered. But Boleslas was still plotting, and in the year 949, he succeeded in having Wenceslas murdered. Today, Wenceslas is remembered as a wise and kind ruler who lived out his Christian faith.

Recipes to share

Good King Wenceslas went out in the bitter cold of winter to bring warmth to the life of a poor peasant. There is something comforting this time of year in a warm cup of "something." Here are some drink mixes that you can mix up and package in decorative containers to share with others during holiday entertaining or as holiday gifts. Young children especially will have fun measuring and mixing the ingredients in these mixes.

Spiced mocha mix

Ingredients:
½ cup instant coffee powder or coffee crystals
½ cup firmly packed dark brown sugar
¼ cup granulated sugar
¼ cup unsweetened cocoa powder
1 teaspoon ground cinnamon
½ teaspoon ground nutmeg

Spiced lemon-ginger tea mix

Ingredients:
1 cup instant tea
1 cup sugar
2 teaspoons ground cloves
2 teaspoons ground ginger
1 teaspoon ground allspice

For both recipes: Combine all ingredients in a medium-size bowl. Spoon the mixture into a container with a tight-fitting lid and store for up to 2 months.

If giving the mix as a gift, add a tag with these directions: Add 3 tablespoons of mix to 8 ounces boiling water. Stir until mix is completely dissolved and enjoy!

Day 22

"While they were there, the time came for the baby to be born." Luke 2:6

The story of "Silent Night"

It was almost Christmas in the village of Oberndorf in Bavaria. The year was 1818 and the organist Franz Gruber was planning to practice the music he would play in church on Christmas Eve.

But try as he might, Franz could not make even a single note come from the pipe organ in the church of St. Nicholas. Franz hurried to tell the priest, Father Joseph Mohr.

"What shall we do?" Franz moaned. "The mice have eaten through the bellows and there is no way to repair the organ in time for Christmas Eve services!"

What can we do? the priest and the organist thought to themselves. Then Father Mohr smiled. "I know," he said to Franz. "We will pray!" Franz Gruber stopped pacing the floor. "Of course," he said. "It is simple! We will pray."

Both men had many things to do in preparation for the Christmas services, so they went about their tasks, not forgetting to pray. Then Father Mohr received news of a call he needed to make—a woodcutter's wife who lived on the edge of the village had just had a baby. The priest hurried out in the snow and cold to welcome and bless the new baby and the woodcutter's family.

As he trudged home from the woodcutter's cottage, Father Mohr thought about the tiny face of the new child as he nestled in his mother's arms. He thought about the joy this gift of new life brought to the family. And he thought about what it would have been like to see the Christ child on that first Christmas Eve long before.

When he returned to his house, Father Mohr wanted to share his feelings with the rest of his people. He sat down with his pen and began to write, and a beautiful poem was formed.

Then Father Mohr hurried to find his friend, Franz Gruber. "Franz, my good friend," the priest said urgently, "please write a tune to go with my new poem. Make it simple enough so that I can sing it with my guitar."

The organist knew the service began in only a short time. But when he read the poem, he knew there would be time enough. Slowly, Franz began to hum a soft melody. Soon both of the men were humming, then singing the words, "Stille Nacht, Heilige Nacht. . . ."

And that is the true story of how the words and music to the hymn "Silent Night" were written many years ago.

Silent Night

1. Si - lent night, ho - ly night, all is calm, all is bright
2. Si - lent night, ho - ly night, shep - herds quake at the sight;
3. Si - lent night, ho - ly night, Son of God, love's pure light

round yon Vir - gin Moth-er and Child. Ho - ly In - fant, so ten-der and mild,
glo - ries stream from heav-en a - far, heav'n-ly hosts__ sing, Al - le - lu - ia,
ra - diant beams from thy ho - ly face, with the dawn of re - deem - ing grace,

sleep in heav - en - ly peace,__ sleep__ in heav - en - ly peace.__
Christ, the Sav - ior, is born!__ Christ,__ the Sav - ior, is born!__
Je - sus, Lord, at thy birth,__ Je - sus, Lord, at thy birth. __

Symbol tree garland

Supplies: Construction paper in a variety of colors; symbol patterns (see pp. 30-31); yarn, string, or ribbon; scissors; pencil; stapler or glue.

If you do not have a garland for your Christmas tree, consider making one of symbol shapes. Fold construction paper in half. Lay your patterns on the paper with the top on the fold. Trace around the pattern and cut out, being careful not to cut through the fold. Hang the symbols over yarn, string, or ribbon. Glue or staple each symbol together, especially near the string, so it will not shift around when the garland is hung on the tree.

Note: You might wish to use heavy metallic giftwrap instead of construction paper, to add a shine to your Christmas tree. If you use giftwrap, it works best to keep your symbol shapes small, to avoid having them curl. A good source for pattern shapes to trace are holiday cookie cutters.

Day 23

"And the glory of the Lord will be revealed, and all mankind together will see it. For the mouth of the Lord has spoken."   Isaiah 40:5

Christmas customs around the world

There are as many different holiday customs as there are countries around the world. Perhaps you and your family celebrate Christmas in a special way that is part of your own ethnic or cultural background. My own family has adapted some customs from our heritage, personalizing them in ways that are special to us. For example, we share the rice pudding and fruit soup that is traditional in Scandinavian homes on Christmas Eve. But in addition to a year of good luck, the person who finds the almond in his or her rice also *makes* a Christmas tree ornament for the next year's lucky person.

A Greek custom is to hide a coin, wrapped in foil or plastic wrap, inside a loaf of homemade bread or coffee cake. The coin is supposed to bring good luck to the person who receives it. It is to be saved, not spent.

In Poland and Czechoslovakia, families share the *oplatki* or *oplatky*, a large white wafer made by monks, that has a holy picture imprinted on it to remind people of the birth of Jesus. One family member begins by breaking the wafer and passing a piece to each person. Then everyone offers their prayers.

Consider adapting a custom from another land for your family. You can find out more about Christmas customs from your local library, and by asking others how they celebrate Christmas.

Crackers

Supplies: Cardboard tubes from paper towels or bathroom tissue; tissue paper, crepe paper, or giftwrap; gum, candy, or other small treats; ribbon.

Crackers are a favorite British Christmas tradition. To make your own, cut paper to fit around the cardboard tube, being sure to leave some of the paper hanging over the ends. Fill the tubes with little treats such as gum, candy, raisins, nuts, or small toys. You might print a favorite Bible verse on a slip of paper to put into the cracker. Some people add a folded paper hat for each person to wear. Wrap the paper around the tube and tie with ribbons as shown. Lay each cracker by someone's plate at mealtime.

Day 24

"And she gave birth to her firstborn, a son. She wrapped him in cloths and placed him in a manger."   Luke 2:7

Disguised gifts

It is believed that the custom of wrapping gifts at Christmas may have originated in Denmark. In that country people still go to great lengths to disguise their gifts with fancy wrappings. Part of the joy of receiving gifts there is in trying to guess what is inside, and a great part in the giving of the gift is in making sure no one can guess what it is!

God's gift to us came disguised too. That baby wrapped in swaddling cloths and lying in a manger was more than he appeared to be. He was the Savior of the world, the King of Kings.

Make-your-own wrapping paper

Supplies: Brown paper bags or mailing paper, shelf paper, or paper of any kind; acrylic or tempera paints; sponges, foam shoe insoles, cork, yarn or string; blocks of wood; scissors; glue.

Cut sponges into the shapes you want, or cut shapes from foam shoe insoles (the kind with holes in them) or cork and glue the cut shapes onto small blocks of wood. Pieces of yarn or string coiled into interesting designs can also be glued to blocks of wood to make printing stamps.

Once you have made your printing stamps, dip them into the paint, blot off the extra, and then make interesting designs on your paper. Let dry and then wrap your gifts!

Here are some other wrapping ideas:

Cut two identical shapes from paper, large enough to cover your gift.

Staple the shapes together along all edges, leaving only enough space open to put the gift inside. Once filled, staple the shape shut. If you like, you can decorate the paper with felt-tip pens before stapling.

Make fabric bags by folding a rectangle of fabric in half and sewing up the sides. This makes a nice reusable gift wrap. Use a pinking shears to trim the top edges before you sew the sides together. Put your gift inside, then gather the top together and tie it closed with a ribbon.

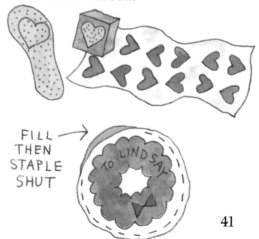

FILL →
THEN
STAPLE
SHUT

TO LINDSAY

Day 25

"The Word became flesh and lived for a while among us. We have seen his glory of the one and only Son, who came from the Father, full of grace and truth."
                                                                      John 1:14

The legend of the orphan's gift

Once upon a time a small orphan boy lived in a village in Europe. It was Christmas time and the village custom was that everyone put gifts under a great Christmas tree standing in the village square. Then on Christmas morning, everyone in the village gathered together around the tree to sing Christmas hymns and give the gifts under the tree to those people who were very poor.

One special Christmas, the boy who was an orphan wanted to leave a gift under the tree. But he didn't have much that he could give. In fact, the only things that the small boy owned were a wagon, a red scarf, and one copper penny.

The boy thought very hard. "I know," he said to himself, "I will leave my wagon under the tree. Even though it is a small wagon, someone would surely find it as useful as I do."

But as the boy pulled his wagon over to put it under the tree, another child put a new shiny wagon there. The boy who was an orphan thought to himself, "My wagon is old and dented—it's rusty and has so many scratches on it. I can't give my wagon as a gift."

And he sadly pulled his wagon away from the tree.

Then he thought, "Maybe someone could use my scarf. Even though it is faded, it still keeps me warm."

So the boy took his scarf off from around his neck and went to put it under the tree. But just as he bent down, another child put a brand-new, soft scarf under the tree.

The boy who was an orphan thought to himself, "My scarf is too old to put under the tree." So he sadly put the scarf back around his neck and walked away. When he put his hands in his pocket, his fingers closed around his copper penny.

Surely someone could use his copper penny, the boy thought. But just as he was putting his copper penny under the Christmas tree, another person placed a chest of gold there.

Now the boy was very sad. "My copper penny is so small," he thought, "no one will even notice it is there. What good is one copper penny next to a chest of gold?"

There didn't seem to be anything that the boy who was an orphan could put under the Christmas tree. As the boy walked slowly home, he heard a choir practicing one of the Christmas hymns they would sing the next morning. The song the choir was singing gave the boy an idea.

The next morning, all the people who lived in the village hurried to the Christmas tree. As they gathered together singing, everyone looked for the gift he or she had put under the tree, hoping that it would be the best gift of all. Everyone noticed the shiny new wagon, the soft scarf, and the chest of gold. But then they noticed something else—one small orphan boy, curled up in a ball under the tree fast asleep.

For you see, the boy had remembered something very important. When God had wanted to give the best gift of all, God gave himself.

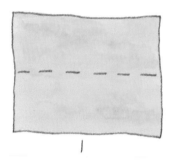

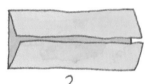

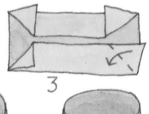

Gifts from the heart

Make one or more of these "gifts from the heart" to frame a personal or family photo for another person.

Folded picture frames

Supplies: Construction paper or other lightweight paper; felt-tip pens; a 3″ photograph.

Cut a piece of paper to measure 8″ x 10″. Fold the paper in half lengthwise, then unfold. Fold the outer edges to the center line. Fold the top layer of each corner back as shown. Turn the paper over and slide one end into the other. Insert a photograph. Use felt-tip pens to decorate the frame.

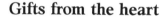

Picture magnets

Supplies: Metal lids from frozen juice concentrate cans; magnet strip; photograph; craft glue or a hot glue gun; assorted ribbons and small artificial flowers to use as trim.

Cut the photograph to fit inside the juice can lid and glue it down. Affix the magnet to the back of the lid with craft glue or a hot glue gun. Arrange ribbons and artificial flowers in a pleasing manner at the top or bottom of the frame and glue in place.

Day 26

"But the eyes of the Lord are on those who fear him, on those whose hope is in his unfailing love." 　　　　　　　　　　　　　　　　*Psalm 33:18*

A promised Savior

For thousands of years the people of God looked for the Savior to come. For generations they prayed that God would deliver them from their enemies. At times God seemed far off, and the people wondered if God heard their cries. Yet always, there were faithful followers who believed that God would keep the covenant made with Abraham. The psalmist wrote, with hope, "The eyes of the Lord are on the righteous and his ears are attentive to their cry." God did not desert the people. At Christmas we celebrate the coming of that Savior promised long ago. At Christmas we witness the fulfillment of God's love.

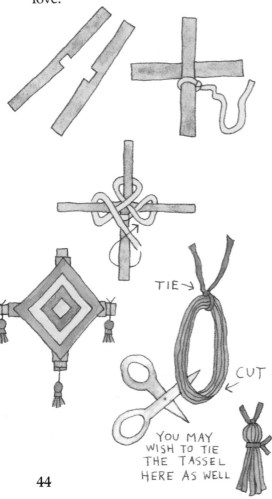

TIE →

CUT ←

YOU MAY
WISH TO TIE
THE TASSEL
HERE AS WELL

Ojos de Dios

Supplies: Two pieces of ¼" dowel, 6"-8" long; yarn in a variety of colors; craft glue or a hot glue gun; scissors.

Ojos de Dios or "God's eye" is a Christmas ornament from Mexico.

To begin, carve out a shallow notch at the center of each dowel. Glue the dowels together at this point.

To wrap, draw the yarn around each arm of the cross in a counter-clockwise (for a right-handed person) direction. The yarn will go over the top of each arm, around the back, then over the top of the next arm. Wrap until the dowels are covered. Change color as you wish, tying the knots in the back so they are not visible.

When finished wrapping, attach tassels to each arm. To make a tassel, wrap yarn around four fingers 35 times. Remove from your hand and tie together at one end. Cut the other end to form the tassel, then tie to the dowels.

Day 27

"Praise the Lord. Praise the Lord from the heavens, praise him in the heights above. . . . Praise the Lord from the earth, you . . . wild animals and all cattle, small creatures and flying birds."
                                                                    Psalm 148:1, 7, 10

The legend of the birds

There are many legends surrounding the first Christmas and the part the birds played in it. The first bird to hear the good news about Jesus' birth was the jet black raven. As the raven flew over the hills of Bethlehem on that first Christmas Eve, the angels appeared in the sky and told him the glorious news. Quickly the raven flew off to share the news he had heard with all of the other birds of the air.

As soon as the stork heard the news, she flew to the stable and plucked the softest feathers from her breast to make a soft, fluffy pillow for the Christ child. The tiny wren wove a blanket from the softest leaves she could find to cover the baby Jesus as he lay in the manger.

The doves nestled in the rafters and cooed a lullaby, and the nightingale sang the loveliest song of all, soothing the new baby into a peaceful sleep.

Care for the birds

St. Francis of Assisi felt that the birds and animals should be remembered in Christmas rejoicing because they were present at Christ's birth.

A feeding tree   Decorate a tree or bush in your yard for the animals to come and eat from. String cranberries, popcorn, miniature marshmallows, and carrot rounds on thread and hang from the tree, either as garlands or in single strings. Spread a thin layer of peanut butter on a pinecone and roll in birdseed, then attach yarn or string to hang it from a tree branch. String peanuts in the shell and hang from the branches.

Squirrel corn   Pound three or four nails through a piece of board, leaving a good portion of the nail sticking up. Push dried corn still on the cob onto the nails and set out for squirrels to eat.

Remember, once you start feeding birds and squirrels, they will depend on you to continue until springtime. Be sure to put clean water out for them as well, especially if you have several days of freezing temperatures.

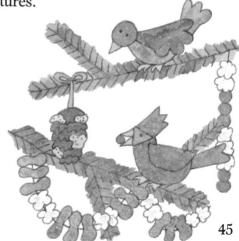

45

Day 28

"The shepherds returned, glorifying and praising God for all the things they had heard and seen, which were just as they had been told." Luke 2:20

The night of nights

The time has finally arrived—Christmas Eve. Tonight families gather at special meals. Many will attend candlelight services. Some families will open their gifts on this night, while others look with eager anticipation to the morning.

It is the night of nights. For a group of shepherds long ago, it was a night that changed their lives. They were greeted by angels with astounding news. A baby was born who was the Son of God. They would find him in a manger. And it was all true.

This amazing news continues to change lives today. Throughout this Advent season, you have read the words of prophecy and love. You have prepared your homes and your hearts for this baby. Now is the time to welcome him with thanks and praise!

"Here is the stable" fingerplay

Here is the stable
(*Form roof's peak with hands.*)
Where Jesus was born
(*Rock imaginary baby in arms.*)
And was laid in the manger
that first Christmas morn.
(*Motion with cupped hands toward floor.*)
And Mary and Joseph
(*Motion to left for Mary, to right for Joseph.*)
And cattle and sheep
(*Indicate horns for cattle; rub lamb's back.*)
Smiled down on the baby
and watched him, asleep.
(*Fold hands and rest cheek on them.*)

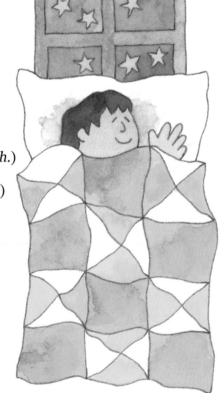

Christmas (December 25)

"Today in the town of David a Savior has been born to you; he is Christ the Lord."

Luke 2:11

The prophecy

It had been many long years since God had promised the people a Messiah, a Savior. God's people waited patiently and prayed diligently that the Messiah would come soon.

One prophet named Isaiah gave God's people these messages:

God wants you to live in peace. God will give you the perfect king to rule over you. This king will come from King David's family and he will have great wisdom and knowledge.

This king will love and obey and praise God more than anything else. He will be a fair judge and will help all of those who need it, even those people that no one else will help.

This king will rule wisely and in peace. During that time, sheep and wolves will live side by side. Calves and lion cubs will eat together and little children will care for them. Cows and bears will live together in peace and even a baby will be able to play safely by a poisonous snake.

The people will see a great light and they will know how to live a peaceful and joyous life. For a child will be born, a son will be given, and the government will be upon his shoulders. He will be called Wonderful Counselor, Mighty God, Everlasting Father, Prince of Peace. He will rule forever.

The annunciation

Mary was a woman who loved God. She was soon to be married to a man named Joseph. Then one day the angel Gabriel came to Mary. At first she was afraid. What could God's angel want with her?

But the angel said, "Mary, do not be afraid! God loves you and is with you. God has something for you to do."

Mary wondered what the angel meant. Surely she was not important enough to do something for God!

"God has blessed you," the angel said. "Even though you are not yet married, you will have a son. Name him Jesus. He will be the Son of God."

"I am the Lord's servant," Mary said. "I will trust in God."

After the angel left Mary, she had many things to think about. She decided to go see her cousin Elizabeth. Mary knew Elizabeth loved God too. She wanted to tell Elizabeth what the angel had said.

When Elizabeth saw Mary coming to her home, she ran to meet her. Elizabeth could tell that Mary had something important to say. "God has blessed you!" Elizabeth said to Mary. And she was happy for Mary. Elizabeth also had some news. She, too, was going to have a baby.

Then Mary sang a beautiful song of praise: "My soul praises and glorifies the Lord, and my spirit rejoices in God my Savior. God has blessed me, a humble servant, with a great and wondrous gift. God remembers the people who love him and will always take care of me!"

Mary stayed with Elizabeth for about three months, because they had many things to talk about.

The birth of Jesus

As the time came closer to the birth of Mary's baby, the ruler from Rome made a decree. "Everyone must travel to their hometowns," Caesar Augustus said. "Everyone must be counted so that I know how many people there are."

Mary and Joseph had to travel to their hometown of Bethlehem. And they didn't have much time to get ready. They packed quickly and set off.

Mary and Joseph were very tired when they finally reached Bethlehem. It was nighttime and they needed to find a place to sleep. But all of the rooms in the town were already full of other people who had come to be counted. There was no room for Mary and Joseph anywhere.

Mary and Joseph tried one more place. But this inn was full too.

"I'm sorry," the innkeeper said. "I have no room in my inn. But you can stay in my stable if you like. It is warm and dry there."

And while Mary and Joseph were there, in the stable, Mary's baby was born. She wrapped the baby in the soft cloths she had brought with her. Then she laid him gently in a manger filled with clean, fresh hay. Mary smiled and said, "His name is Jesus."

The shepherds and the angels

That same night, there were shepherds watching over their flocks on the hillside. From the hillside, the shepherds could see a few lights twinkling in the town of Bethlehem.

But suddenly there was a great light! This light was so bright, the shepherds had to put their hands over their faces.

Then an angel of the Lord appeared to them and said, "Don't be afraid! I bring you good news of great joy! Tonight, in the little town of Bethlehem, a baby was born. This baby is God's Son. He is sleeping in a manger."

Then an even greater light appeared in the sky and there were many angels singing, "Glory to God in the highest! And peace to God's people on earth."

As the angel's voices faded away, the bright light disappeared. "Let's go to Bethlehem!" the shepherds said. "We can find this baby who is God's Son and worship him."

So the shepherds hurried to the stable where Mary and Joseph and baby Jesus were. And after they saw the baby in the manger, the shepherds told everyone they met what they had seen and heard that night.

A visit from the wise men

When Jesus was born in Bethlehem, wise men who lived in a faraway country saw a new star in the sky. Each man studied the star carefully to see what it could mean. And each man thought to himself, "This new star is so bright it must mean something special. It must mean that a new king has been born. I will follow the star and find the king so I can worship him."

The wise men thought carefully about what kind of gifts they could take to a newborn king. One wise man thought, "I will take the new king a gift of gold. Gold is a gift for a king."

Another wise man decided, "I will take the new king a gift of incense. Incense is a gift for a king."

And another wise man thought, "I will take the new king a gift of myrrh. Myrrh is a gift for a king."

After they had gathered their gifts, the wise men began their journey to find the new king. The wise men followed the bright star in the sky for many days and many nights, until finally they came to Jerusalem. There they asked everyone they saw, "Where is the new king? We saw the bright new star in the sky and we have come to worship the new king."

When King Herod heard that there were wise men looking for a new king, he was surprised. Did they know something he didn't know? Herod asked the wisest men in his kingdom who the strangers were talking about. They told him that the prophets long ago had said a new king would be born in Bethlehem.

King Herod met with the wise men and told them he thought a new king would be born in Bethlehem. "Find the new king," Herod told the men, "and tell me where he is. Then I can go and worship him too."

The wise men followed the star to Bethlehem until it stopped over the place where Mary and Joseph and baby Jesus were.

The wise men were so happy when they saw the new baby. They gave him their gifts of gold, incense, and myrrh, and they worshiped him.

But the wise men did not go back to King Herod and tell him where the new king was. God warned them in a dream to go home by another way.

The escape to Egypt

After the wise men had gone an angel of the Lord appeared to Joseph in a dream and told him, "King Herod is looking for your child. Get up and take Mary and Jesus away to Egypt."

So Joseph got up and woke Mary. "Come," he said, "we must take our son Jesus and travel to Egypt. It will be safer for us there."

That night, Mary and Joseph and baby Jesus left Bethlehem and traveled safely to Egypt. And they stayed there until Herod had died.

EPIPHANY

History and traditions

At the time that Christianity became the religion of the Roman Empire, the twelve days between December 25 and January 6 were known as the "Twelve Holy Days." This time was also known as the "Twelve Holy Nights" or "Christmastide." Today we call it the season of Christmas.

January 6 also has many names, including Epiphany, Twelfth Night and Three King's Day. This day and its religious festivities celebrate or commemorate three great events in Jesus' life—his baptism in the Jordan, the visit of the wise men, and the first recorded miracle of Jesus, the changing of water into wine at the wedding in Cana.

The Christian season of Epiphany is even older than the celebration of Christmas. *Epiphany* means "manifestation" or "appearance," and the day of Epiphany was originally celebrated in honor of Jesus' baptism in the River Jordan, when a dove descended from heaven and landed on Jesus, and he heard the words "This is my Beloved Son." At that time, God became "manifest" in Jesus Christ.

The season of Epiphany lasts until Ash Wednesday, and it serves as a bridge between the birth of Jesus and his passion. Since about the fifth century A.D., Christians around the world have observed this season of the church year as the time when the wise men visited the Son of God.

In addition, Epiphany is rich with the symbolism of light brought into the world through Jesus Christ. Stars are one of the major symbols that represent the season of Epiphany.

As the wise men traveled from far-off lands to see the new king and then returned to tell others of what they had seen, so we are reminded during Epiphany of our mission to "go and make disciples" and to share the good news with people everywhere.

First Day of Christmas

"Where is the one who has been born king of the Jews? We saw his star in the east and have come to worship him."   *Matthew 2:2*

Boxing Day and the Feast of Stephen, December 26

In Great Britain, Canada, and Australia, December 26 is called "Boxing Day." During the Middle Ages, it was the custom on this day for those people who were wealthy to share with those who were poor. Usually a "poor box" was left in the church for people's donations. The money collected was shared with people in need. Another custom of "boxing" was to give a small gift of money to someone who had been of service to you during the year. In early times, the lords of the manors gave gifts to their servants on this day. Nowadays gifts may be shared with the mail carrier, delivery persons, or employees.

Today, many people also observe Boxing Day by attending special dramatic performances or sporting events.

It is also a day when people begin to take stock of their good fortune in the past year, and their hopes, goals, and dreams for the year to come.

The Feast of Stephen, also celebrated on December 26, was once a very important religious holiday. The day after Jesus' birth was chosen to honor Stephen, the first Christian who was willing to give his life for his belief in Jesus as God's Son.

Family hope chest

Supplies: Small box, such as a shoe box; shelf paper or giftwrap (something with stars on it is appropriate); small pieces of note paper (at least one piece for each family member); pencils; felt-tip markers.

Create a family hope chest and begin now to look ahead to the new year.

If you wish, draw designs and symbols on the shelf paper with felt-tip markers. You might include symbols appropriate for the upcoming Epiphany season. Then cover the box with the paper. Cut a slot in the top of the box.

Have each family member write down one hope he or she has for the coming year. You might put it in the form of a prayer, or in the form of a resolution for the new year. Then put all the slips in the box. On New Year's Eve or New Year's Day, open the box and share your hopes and prayers with one another.

Second Day of Christmas

"My eyes have seen your salvation, which you have prepared in the sight of all people, a light for revelation to the Gentiles and for glory to your people Israel."
Luke 2:30-32

Simeon and Anna

When Jesus was about forty days old, Mary and Joseph took him to the temple in Jerusalem, as God's law instructed them to do. It was while they were there that Simeon, a righteous and devout man of God, came and took the child in his arms and began to praise God. It had been revealed to Simeon that he would not die before he saw the promised Messiah. His words caused Mary and Joseph to marvel. But Simeon knew this baby was the Son of God.

Then a prophetess named Anna, a very old woman who never left the temple, but spent her days praying and fasting, approached them and gave thanks and praise. And she spread the word about the child to all she saw.

And Joseph and Mary returned with the child to Galilee and their own town of Nazareth.

Glitter stars

Supplies: Assorted colors of glitter; wax paper; white craft glue; shoebox lid; fishing line or thread.

Line the shoebox lid with wax paper, then draw star shapes with glue on the paper. The glue lines should be somewhat thick, rather than narrow. Sprinkle glitter over the glue, making sure it is completely covered. Remove the wax paper from the shoebox lid, shaking excess glitter back into the container. Let the stars dry for about 48 hours, then carefully peel the wax paper away, working from each star point. You can hang the stars with nylon fishing line or thread to make a ceiling full of stars.

Third Day of Christmas

"On coming to the house, they saw the child with his mother Mary, and they bowed down and worshiped him. Then they opened their treasures and presented him with gifts of gold and of incense and of myrrh."

Matthew 2:11

The legend of rosemary

This is the legend about the rosemary plant and how it became the fragrant herb that we know today.

When Mary and Joseph and the donkey and baby Jesus were traveling to Egypt, they stopped by a small stream to rest. Mary and Joseph knelt by the stream to give thanks to God for guiding them.

Then Mary washed the soft cloths she had wrapped baby Jesus in in the stream. When she looked around for a place to dry them, Mary noticed the sturdy rosemary plant.

"This will be a good place for the soft cloths to dry," Mary said as she hung them carefully over the branches.

In the warm sun the cloths dried quickly. The warm sun also caused the plant to give off a fragrance that made the air smell good. When Mary lifted the dry cloths from the plant, they smelled as delightful as the air.

"Thank you," Mary whispered to the plant. "From now on I will call you Mary's Rose."

As Mary leaned over the plant for one last smell of its sweetness, she held the baby Jesus in her arms. When he reached out his hand to touch the plant, small blue flowers burst forth on the plant. The blue flowers were the same color as Mary's robe, and we now call this herb rosemary.

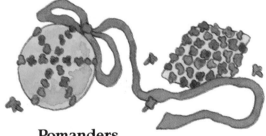

Pomanders

Supplies: Apples, oranges, or lemons; whole cloves; a knitting needle or bamboo skewer; small hammer; pencil; orris root powder.

Outline with a pencil a design that you would like to make on a piece of fruit, or determine a starting point if you would like to cover the whole piece. Poke holes into the fruit with a knitting needle or skewer, then insert one whole clove into each hole. You may want to use the hammer to secure the clove in the hole. Roll the completed fruit in orris root powder to help preserve it. Roll the fruit in the powder several times a day, and set it in a well-ventilated place to cure. Attach a length of ribbon for hanging once the fruit becomes somewhat darkened.

Fourth Day of Christmas

"An angel of the Lord appeared to Joseph in a dream. 'Get up,' he said, "take the child and his mother and escape to Egypt. Stay there until I tell you, for Herod is going to search for the child to kill him.' " Matthew 2:13

The legend of the donkey

When Mary and Joseph and the donkey and baby Jesus left for Egypt, they had to travel quickly. An angel had warned Joseph in a dream that King Herod was looking for the baby and wanted to kill him.

But Mary and Joseph were tired. So many things happened to them in such a short time. When Joseph found a sheltered spot where they could rest, he built a small fire and they all lay down to sleep.

But the donkey didn't sleep. In the distance, he could hear the sound of the King's soldiers searching for the baby. The donkey tried to nudge Mary awake. He neighed several times to wake Joseph. But the donkey's voice was too soft and Mary and Joseph were too tired to hear him.

The donkey knew that when the soldiers got closer, they would be able to see the glow of the fire. Finally, the donkey made the loudest noise he could— *HEE-HAW!*

That noise woke Joseph quickly. He heard how close the soldiers were and put the fire out. When Herod's soldiers passed by, they didn't see the family huddled in the dark.

Now when people hear the donkey's loud *HEE-HAW,* they remember how the donkey who carried Mary on his back saved baby Jesus from King Herod's soldiers.

Tin can lanterns

Supplies: Small empty tin cans; water; nail; hammer; votive candle.

Fill a small tin can (large enough to hold your candle) with water and freeze the water until it is solid. Use a hammer and nail to punch the design into the can. (The ice will give you something solid to pound against.) Let the ice melt. Dry the can and set your votive candle inside.

Glitter candles

Supplies: Candles; assorted colors of glitter; towels.

Dampen a towel with hot water, then roll the candle in it. After a moment, check the wax to see if it is somewhat softened. When it is, roll the candle in the glitter. The wax will be softened enough for the glitter to stick to it, making an elegant candle.

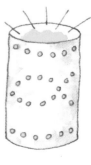

Fifth Day of Christmas

"So he got up, took the child and his mother during the night and left for Egypt."
                                                                    Matthew 2:14

The legends of On

Egyptians were known as wise people, but at the time of Jesus' birth, many of the wisest people were gone. Only a few sage-priests lived quietly near the ruins of an old temple, Heliopolis, or as the Bible calls it, On.

Also near this temple lived a group of very religious people who worked as gardeners for the wealthy Egyptian merchants and noblemen. Legends tell us that it was here that Joseph and Mary and the donkey and baby Jesus came to escape King Herod.

The On of Bible times still exists in Egypt today. And in the center of the village, there is a tree more than 2000 years old. This tree is called "Mary's tree."

Legends and stories tell us that this was the place where Jesus spent the first years of his life, most likely playing in the shade of "Mary's tree."

Firestarters

Supplies: Old wax candles, crayons, or blocks of paraffin wax; an old muffin tin; paper muffin cups; string; scissors; pinecones; a double boiler made from a saucepan and a large metal can (such as a coffee can).

Cut the string into pieces approximately 6″ long. You will need one for each firestarter.

Carefully melt the wax you are using in the coffee can set in a saucepan of water. As the wax begins to melt, place paper muffin cups into the muffin tin, setting one length of string in the bottom of each, and allowing it to hang out over the edge of the cup.

When the wax is melted, carefully pour it into the muffin cups, filling the cups ½ full. Set a pinecone in the center of each muffin cup and let the wax harden.

Place the finished firestarters in a basket near your fireplace or woodstove and use them with kindling to get your fire started. Just light the string and watch the glow begin!

Sixth Day of Christmas

"But may all who seek you rejoice and be glad in you; may those who love your salvation always say, 'The Lord be exulted!' "　　　　　*Psalm 40:16*

The legend of Baboushka

There is a legend that tells about a woman named Baboushka. Baboushka lived in a village in Russia. Everyone in the village knew that Baboushka's house was the cleanest, her cakes and cookies were the best-tasting, and Baboushka was the *busiest* woman in the entire village.

One day three strangers came to town. They were following a star they said would lead them to the place where a new king had been born. When they needed a place to stay for the night, everyone in the village told them to stay with Baboushka.

Baboushka was pleased to have guests in her home. It wasn't often that she had someone to share her clean home with or to cook her cakes and cookies for.

As the three strangers sat eating, they talked of their search for the new king. They were eager to find him to give him their gifts and to worship him. "We are leaving the first thing in the morning, Baboushka," the strangers said. "Come with us to find the new king!"

"We'll see," Baboushka said to the strangers as she swept the kitchen floor.

After the strangers had gone to sleep for the night, Baboushka kept working. There was so much work to do to keep a clean house!

When morning came, it seemed that Baboushka had just fallen asleep. The strangers tried to wake her, but Baboushka murmured, "I'll catch up with you. I must get a little more sleep." And so the strangers left without her.

When Baboushka finally woke up, it was getting dark. "Oh dear!" Baboushka thought. "I will never find the strangers now."

Quickly Baboushka wrapped some cakes and cookies to take with her on her journey. She went to a special cupboard and took out some toys she had made long ago for another baby. These would be her gifts to the new baby who was born to be king.

Baboushka hurried out into the twilight. She asked everyone she met, "Have you seen three strangers pass this way? They are following a star and I need to catch up with them!" But no one had seen the three strangers. And so Baboushka began her own journey, looking for the star and the strangers who were following it. Some people say Baboushka is still searching for the baby who was born to be king.

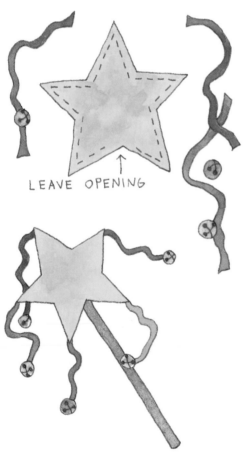

LEAVE OPENING

Star wands

Supplies: Metallic fabric; polyester fiberfill; thread; one 18" length of dowel (per wand); assorted ribbons in rainbow colors; pencil; paper; craft glue or hot glue gun; jingle bells.

Make a star pattern approximately 6" across the widest part. With right sides of the fabric facing, cut two stars, making sure to add a 5/8" seam allowance. Sew the star shape together, leaving an opening about 2" long, for stuffing purposes. Trim the seam, and turn the star right side out, using a pencil to gently push the points all the way out. Stuff the star with the polyester fiberfill so that it is firm, then hand sew the opening shut, leaving just enough room to insert glue and the end of the dowel. Be sure to push the dowel in far enough so that is secure.

Sew jingle bells to the ends of the ribbons and attach to each of the star's points.

Seventh Day of Christmas

"On the eighth day, when it was time to circumcise him, he was named Jesus, the name the angel had given him before he had been conceived."

Luke 2:21

"Jesus Day," January 1

January 1 is the beginning of a new year. There are New Year's celebrations around the world, and people take time to reflect on what they hope to achieve or accomplish in the coming year. This day is also traditional for making New Year's resolutions or a list of things that you may want to change about yourself and the way you live.

January 1 is also "Jesus Day." It is a day to reflect on the gift of love that God gave us in Jesus and a time to realize anew how much Jesus loved us, that he would sacrifice his life for us.

Take the time as a family to do a Bible study, looking up the different names and references for Jesus in your Bible. A concordance is a good place to start. See how many you can list on a sheet of paper and use these names in your prayers throughout the coming year.

Jesus mobile

Supplies: Assorted colors of poster board or construction paper; dowel; paper hole punch; yarn or thread.

Refer to the symbols on pages 30-31 and choose the ones that you feel mean most represent Jesus. Cut these symbols from paper and cut the letters in the name *JESUS* from paper as well. Follow the diagram for a suggested way to punch holes in both the symbols and letters and hang them from a dowel to create a mobile. Hang the completed mobile where it will blow gently in the breeze.

Eighth Day of Christmas

"When they saw the star, they were overjoyed." Matthew 2:10

The legend of the apple star

Once there was a child who wondered where the stars went in the daytime. He asked Grandmother, "Where do the stars go when the sun comes out?"

Grandmother smiled and said, "Each star lives in a little red house with no doors or windows. If you go outside, you might be able to find one."

So the child began searching for the star's little red house.

When the child met a black cat, he asked, "Have you seen a little red house with no doors and no windows that has a star inside?"

"No," said the cat. "Maybe the yellow duck has seen the little red house you are looking for."

So the child went to the duck pond and asked the yellow duck, "Have you seen a little red house with no doors or windows but with a star inside?"

"No," said the yellow duck. "But maybe the bluebird in that tree has seen the house you are looking for."

So the child looked up in the tree where the bluebird was sitting and said, "I am looking for a little red house with no doors or windows but with a star inside. Have you seen it?"

"Yes," said the bluebird. "I have seen the house you are looking for. In fact, the little red house is here in this tree!"

So the child looked up and guess what he saw? A red apple. *(Cut a red apple crosswise and see the star formed on the inside by the seeds.)*

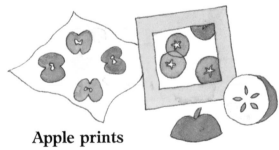

Apple prints

Supplies: Apples; pie tins or shallow bowls; acrylic or tempera paints; knives; paper or muslin squares; newspaper.

Spread newspaper on your workspace. Pour the paints into the pie tins or bowls. Cut the apples, either crossways or from the stem to bottom to make your prints. Press the apple halves into the paint, then press firmly onto the paper or fabric.

If you are using fabric and acrylic paints, you might want to make potholders or another useable item from the muslin pieces. To set the paint, put the fabric piece in the clothes-dryer on HIGH for 10 minutes, then complete the item.

Ninth Day of Christmas

"May you be blessed by the Lord, the Maker of heaven and earth."

Psalm 115:15

Time to go a-wassailing!

It is traditional to toast the end of the holiday season by drinking to the health of loved ones and friends and asking God's blessings on the coming year. The English Wassail bowl is one of the most colorful and well-known toasting customs.

The word *wassail* comes from a Norse phrase *ves weill* which means "to be in health." Although there are many variations of the wassail punch, it is usually a hot spiced cider with a fruity apple base.

In England, in times past, the village wassail bowl was carried from home to home, with everyone helping themselves to a steaming cupful. The remainder of the punch was often poured through the roots of an apple tree and a shotgun was fired through the tree's branches in hopes that the apple harvest would be good in the coming year.

Spiced cider mix

Ingredients:
½ cup sugar
1 orange peel, scored and peeled into long strips
2 teaspoons whole cloves
1 teaspoon whole allspice
2 cinnamon sticks, broken into pieces

Combine all ingredients and mix thoroughly. Pour the mixture into a 6" square of doubled cheesecloth or muslin. Tie the fabric closed with a ribbon and attach a tag with these brewing instructions: To serve the spiced cider, combine the contents of this bag with 4 cups of apple cider in a saucepan or crockpot. Bring to a boil, then reduce heat. Cover and simmer for 30 minutes, then remove the muslin bag. Strain if necessary and serve warm. Makes 1 quart.

Tenth day of Christmas

"After Jesus was born in Bethlehem in Judea, during the time of King Herod, Magi from the east came to Jerusalem." Matthew 2:1

The wise men

January 6 is known as Three King's Day in many countries. On this day, people often attend a special parade where the three kings ride camels.

In most countries where people speak Spanish, children receive gifts from three kings rather than from Saint Nicholas or Santa Claus at Christmas.

Children in other countries often make parades of their own, with each small group led by a child who carries a star on a pole. Usually the person who carries the star is dressed to represent one of the three kings.

Even though the Bible does not tell us much about the wise men, people through the ages have wondered and imagined how these strangers from a far off land traveled to worship the newborn king.

Try making these stars as reminders of the gifts the wise men brought to Jesus and the light that Jesus brings to all people.

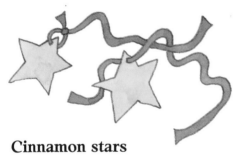

Cinnamon stars

Supplies: 1 cup of ground cinnamon; 4 tablespoons white craft glue; ¾ to 1 cup water; rolling pin; star-shaped cookie cutter; baking sheet; straws; wax paper; ribbon.

Stir the cinnamon, glue, and water together to make a dough the consistency of cookie dough. Refrigerate the dough for about 2 hours.

Sprinkle cinnamon on your work surface. Spoon the chilled dough onto the cinnamon and knead the dough until it is smooth. Sprinkle more cinnamon as you need it, to keep the dough from sticking.

Roll the dough to about ¼" thickness and cut out star shapes with a cookie cutter.

To dry the stars, lay them on wax paper and let them stay at room temperature, turning them twice a day for about four days. If you want to speed up the drying time, bake the stars on a baking sheet in a warm oven for 2 hours, checking often to be sure they do not burn.

Before the stars are completely dry, poke a hole in each where you want to attach a piece of yarn or ribbon for hanging.

Hang your stars on different lengths of ribbon in a window in your house to remind you of the bright morning star, the light of the world, the Son of God.

Eleventh day of Christmas

"From the fullness of his grace we have all received one blessing after another."

John 1:16

Untrimming the tree

The Christmas tree was traditionally left up in the home until January 6, the day of Epiphany. At that time, the family untrimmed the tree, putting away all of their Christmas decorations and trimmings.

This year as you take down your tree, think about its significance. The evergreen is a symbol of everlasting life, the gift that we have as followers of Jesus Christ.

Tree cross

If you have a natural Christmas tree, you and your family might want to cut off some of the branches, forming two of them into a cross to hang in your home until the next season of the church year, Lent. During the season of Lent you can adorn it with a crown of thorns. On Palm Sunday, decorate it with palm branches. During Holy Week, drape it with a black veil. And on Easter Sunday cover it with flowers.

The Day of Epiphany

"Arise, shine, for your light has come, and the glory of the Lord rises upon you. See, darkness covers the earth and the thick darkness is over the peoples, but the Lord rises upon you and his glory appears over you. Nations will come to your light, and kings to the brightness of your dawn."

Isaiah 60:1-3

Twelfth Night

You are probably familiar with the Christmas carol about the twelve days of Christmas. During earlier times in England, people continued their Christmas celebrations for twelve days, from Christmas Day until Epiphany on January 6.

January 6, the Twelfth Night, was the day with the biggest celebration of all. There were parties and music, dancing and eating to celebrate the joy of Christmas and Christ's birth. Sometimes a Twelfth Night King or Queen was chosen to preside over the festivities or families, or families shared a favorite family cake recipe as their Twelfth Night Cake. Whoever found the dried bean or pea baked into the cake batter was crowned the king or queen of Twelfth Night. You and your family might want to adapt one of these customs and make your own Twelfth Night/Epiphany celebration.

My gift to Jesus

During the past days of Advent and Christmas, you have thought about God's greatest gift to you—the gift of his Son, Jesus. Make this twelfth day of Christmas one where you think about a gift you can give to Jesus.

The love you have for Jesus is perhaps the greatest gift you can give. And your love for Jesus will spill over into all parts of your life, shaping everything that you do and say, and sharing the good news of God's love and the gift of eternal life with people throughout the world.

64